THE AMERICAN DREAM FOR IMMIGRANT ENTREPRENEURS

THE AMERICAN DREAM FOR IMMIGRANT ENTREPRENEURS

A Beginner's Guide To Freedom, Fame And Fortune In The USA

MOHAMED RACHADI, PH.D.

The American Dream For Immigrant Entrepreneurs
A Beginner's Guide To Freedom, Fame And Fortune In The USA

Copyright ©2018 by Mohamed Rachadi, Ph.D.
All rights reserved.

Published by Rebel Press
Austin, TX
www.RebelPress.com

No part of this publication may be reproduced, stored in a retrieval system, or transmitted in any form or by any means—electronic, mechanical, photocopy, recording, or any other—without the prior permission of the author.

ISBN: 978-1-64339-918-8

Printed in the United States of America

I dedicate this book to my late mother Al Hajja Arbia Bent El Ague. This strong lady raised all six of us after my father died at an early age. She did not read or write any language, but she made sure all of us went to school and received advanced degrees. She is my rock.

I equally dedicate this book to my family members, whom I love dearly, and who encouraged me to write-My wife Connie, my two daughters Ashley Nicole and Jaclyn Michelle, my brothers and sisters.

I dedicate this book to my follow immigrants who face many sacrifices and challenges when they leave their homeland for a new land. They make the journey in search of something new and much better than what they leave behind. They want to be better and make this world a better place by sharing and caring.

"I believe in America."
—Mario Puzo, The Godfather

"Remember, remember always, that all of us, you and I especially, are descended from immigrants and revolutionists."
—Franklin D. Roosevelt

TABLE OF CONTENTS

Acknowledgements xv
Chapter 1   Introduction 1
Chapter 2   Developing the Right Mindset 9
Chapter 3   Setting Goals and Chasing Outcomes 17
Chapter 4   Mastering the English Language 23
Chapter 5   The Innocence of Youth 35
Chapter 6   Be Ready to Give More 51
Chapter 7   Recap: The American Dream for Immigrant Entrepreneurs 61
Chapter 8   Get to Work 71
Chapter 9   Time to Thrive 83
Epilogue   A Letter to a Friend 93
Online Resources for Immigrant Entrepreneurs to the US 101

THE AMERICAN DREAM
— FOR —
IMMIGRANT ENTREPRENEURS

ACKNOWLEDGEMENTS

This work is the culmination of years of experience, acquired expertise and support from so many people and sources that my God had sent my way during this magical and extraordinary life of mine.

I feel blessed and grateful to God first and always for the many second chances I was given after several life threatening accidents and incidents on the road and in hospitals. Every day I thrive to live the life God wants me to live by doing his work and making a difference in the lives of others.

My work would not have been possible without the love and support of my wife and two daughters, siblings and mentors. Mom, dad and brother Abdelkarim, I miss you and will always make you proud.

To all people who touched my life, one time or another, and made it better each day, no matter how small or big the contribution, I salute you and thank you from the bottom of my heart. I will always be grateful for your generosity, your love and friendship. Special thanks to late Monsignor Kaiser and his staff (Catholic Relief Services) for arranging my journey to the

USA and for showing me the way to give without ever asking for anything in return. Special thanks also to the late Mrs. Doris Patterson (Rochester NY) whom I met while I was a student at St. John Fisher College. I helped clear her driveway of many inches of snow, and she became a second mother to me. She did so much for me. She is now an angel who still looks after me from above.

The only way to remember many others, and I don't want to forget anyone or anything, and acknowledge all contributors and their contribution to my life, is to do it by major periods.

After Retirement (2017 - Present)

After my retirement from the corporate world, I embraced the social media universe which opened a whole new world for me by renewing old friendships and finding many new ones from all over the globe. This work would not have been possible without the help from many friends and acquaintances from GoRead, Talk Fusion, Enagic and from so many groups on Facebook and other social media platforms. Special recognition to Ken Dunn and his team at GoRead for introducing me to writing books. Also to one of his mentors and a great writer and speaker himself, Nicholas Boothman, for his friendship, humour, generous time and advice to me and many others. Nicholas Boothman suggested the subtitle for my book *A Beginner's Guide To Fame, Freedom and Fortune*. For their inspiration and generosity, I acknowledge the many leaders at Talk Fusion.

My Years in Business

After completing many years in graduate school, I was blessed to move to California where I landed several jobs with small, medium and large corporations. I learned so much from my colleagues, the customers I had the privilege of serving and the many friends from suppliers and distributors in the Pest Management and Green Industries, with whom I interacted on a daily basis. In my book, I share some of the precious and priceless business fundamentals I learned while working with companies or running my own businesses in Connecticut and Georgia. As an employee and as a business owner, I had the opportunity to visit and enjoy the beauty of many states in the USA and also some other countries. I remained grateful for the many employers, channel partners and customers who provided me with many precious opportunities to learn and earn-Cline Buckner, Waterbury Companies, WHITMIRE Research Laboratories, Target Specialty Products, Van Waters & Rodgers (UNIVAR), Speckoz, Prokoz, UPMA LABS, Morach Regulatory, Brandt, Interstellar Technologies and Rachadi Associates. I will always be grateful to my many mentors who encouraged me and showed me what it takes to succeed in business and in life.

The School Years

As a student, in many places and at different times, I had the pleasure of meeting some of the most wonderful and generous people on earth. To all my teachers/professors, my fellow schoolmates, my students and all staff I met during my time at the institutions listed below, I say thank you for helping me grow up to always do the right things in life.

Concord Law School (Kaplan)
Fordham University
St John Fisher College
New York Business School

ENFA
CIDERA-Jésuite Agricultural School
LYCÉE MOULAY YOUSSEF
TEMARA Elementary

The Innocent Years

And finally, this work will not have been possible without the support, the Love and the friendship from many friends and relatives, from Temara and Sidi Slimane (Morocco). Growing up among them and sharing happy and not so happy moments has left me with so many memories that I will carry with me forever and ever. May God bless us all and bless this beautiful universe. We need each other to make it a better place for the many generations to come.

CHAPTER 1

Introduction

Hello, friend.

More than one million immigrants migrate to the United States of America every year. If you are one of them, this book is for you.

My name is Mohamed Rachadi. I am a 68-year-old immigrant and a naturalized citizen of the United States of America. Over 48 years living in this land, I have been a student, an employee, a taxpayer, a homeowner, and a business owner.

I met my wife, Connie, in 1979, and we got married in 1983. We have two beautiful daughters—Ashley Nicole, 29, and Jaclyn Michelle, 25. They are both single, working, and paying taxes.

I have lived in 4 different states and visited 48. I am passionate about sharing my life experiences in the United States with other immigrants and their families. I have long wanted to write a book with specific guidelines to help immigrants who want to migrate to the United States of America realize the American Dream and their own pursuit of happiness. My intention was to create a book that will help any immigrant from any country transition smoothly from their homeland to the new land.

This book stands out from others on this topic because it offers specific steps applicable to immigrants from all walks of life. Other books or guides for immigrants often cover historical facts, usually about specific ethnic groups which limit readership; for example, a book about Italians, Irish, or other immigrants from specific countries. My book is written to address common, everyday challenges, offering specific and detailed solutions to anyone coming to study or to work and live permanently, regardless of country of origin, religion, political orientations, or socioeconomic class. This book tells the real stories of everyday Americans living and working in the USA, providing the immigrant reader with a realistic view of what to expect when they decide to make the journey to America.

My intention is to help better prepare immigrants headed to the United States to study and go back home—or to work and live permanently in the USA.

Things Do Happen for a Reason

It was late in the summer of 1969 when I learned my life was going to change forever. I had just finished my secondary education at an Agricultural school in Morocco, run by French Jesuits. During the graduation ceremony, I remember vividly the Lebanese Ambassador to Morocco presenting me with a beautiful, expensive looking pen as a reward for my recognition, along with the "Premier Prix D'Excellence"—the highest reward category in my class.

He shook my hand and said in his Lebanese French accent, "*Mes félicitations jeune homme. Votre vie est devant vous et vous irez loin.*" The English translastion: "My congratulations, young man. Your whole life is ahead of you and you will go far."

At that time, I had no idea what it meant. Following graduation, I was offered the opportunity to travel to the United States to study medicine. I did not speak a word of English at that time.

The only thing I knew about America was the movie *West Side Story* that was playing in a movie theater in Rabat, the capital of Morocco.

Monsignor Kaiser of Catholic Relief Services invited me and other friends to the movie that was playing in French. After the movie, I fell in love with the American idea and the way of life presented by the movie. I was determined to pursue the opportunity to travel to the United States to study. By the way, I have now seen *West Side Story* so many times; even my wife and daughters enjoy watching it with me sometimes.

Traveling to the US as a student is not as easy as it sounds. To obtain a student visa, it takes considerable time to apply. You also have to have physicals and many other requirements before you are allowed to travel.

Luckily for me, a representative of Catholic Relief Services worked closely with the American Embassy in Rabat on my behalf and handled all the requirements. The plan was to travel to New York City in September 1969. That did not happen. During my last year at the Jesuit Agricultural school, I was diagnosed with a mild case of tuberculosis and had to spend several months at the hospital.

Although I was cleared by the medical chief, Madame Papillon, a friend of the Jesuits and head of the hospital in Rabat, I had to wait another year before I could travel to New York. That was my first encounter with immigration to the United States of America, and I learned to appreciate what it takes before you are qualified to travel to the U.S.

I felt very defeated. I recall thinking, now what? What am I going to do for a whole year?

Fortunately, the Moroccan government, with the help of the Jesuits, gave me an excellent option through a scholarship—traveling to France to study advanced agriculture. The requirements to travel to France were not as strict as the requirements for the U.S. I was fluent in French and had already traveled to France many times before during the previous few summers. I lived with French families on farms and learned practical aspects of French Agriculture. Time was running out. I had to hurry up and take the flight to Toulouse, France, where I was going to attend an Agricultural school for nine months.

The months flew by, and before I knew it, the day had finally come to begin my new life across the ocean. September 9, 1970 was the day I had long been waiting for. I said goodbye to my mother, my three brothers, my two sisters, and a few friends and relatives who came to wish me a good trip to another world. New York City, here I come!

A Note to the Reader

Every immigrant experience is unique. My intention with this book is not to provide a comprehensive recounting of the immigration story for every individual; rather, my goal is to illuminate some lessons for future immigrants to this great country based on my own personal story.

By following the steps in this book, the reader will realize his or her dreams sooner than later by assimilating and adapting quickly to life in America, living happily ever after in the new homeland.

I believe that I have acquired something of an expertise in the American Dream—after all, I have lived my own over the past 48 years.

This is a complex, multi-faceted society. America is much more than the images you see beamed into your television set from halfway around the world. America is much more than Coca-Cola and Facebook, much more than Trump and Obama. Yes, this is a country that prides itself on capitalism and working hard. But the American experience is fundamentally about a few key ideas—freedom, democracy, and the pursuit of happiness. But these are the qualities that are truly priceless.

One needs to think about what these words mean to appreciate them. It is only after so many years in this country, fully immersed in my "newfound" community, that I can say the following to my fellow immigrants and to my countrymen and countrywomen: the American Dream is a gift to those who embrace it, love it, and live it.

Yes, the price is high. Opportunity is widespread, but not perfectly. Opportunity abounds, but equality of outcomes is far from assured. But even the failures are ultimately worth every single penny and every single tear.

This is how I feel about it. I was searching for a purpose in my life on earth. With the help of God and my loved ones, I found it in sharing and caring-giving back to the community, the country, and the world. This book represents the fruit and the essence of the purpose I found: sharing what I know about the precious life in the United States of America with the millions of immigrants who have been inoculated with the American Dream Spirit and will go through a lot to get here. This book is my gift to my fellow immigrants.

This book is for you. For the dream you harbor in your heart and your soul. For the sacrifices you are willing to make and the challenges you will go through to pursue the dream and the happiness that comes with it. The American Dream is not perfect because perfection is not of this world. The American Dream is simply the best there is, close to perfection.

Over the course of this book, I will address a wide range of topics: helping the reader develop the right mindset about migrating to America, settings goals, the importance of learning the English language for better communication, sharing ideas about the innocence of youth, and how to learn from others without judging. We will examine the art of giving to the community and the country, sharing real, practical ideas about how to adapt and thrive one day at a time. We will cover how you can get started building your dream—not just surviving in America but thriving.

You have already taken major steps in your American journey by picking up this book. I am proud of you.

My promise to you, my reader, is this: After reading this book, you will have learned precious, practical knowledge on how to prepare for the journey to America and how to transition from living in your homeland to living in the new land. You will gain insights on how to survive and thrive during and after the journey to realize your dream—and how you also can live happily ever after in the new homeland.

I am going to keep my promise to my reader by delivering step-by-step guidance that will lead the reader to realizing the American Dream and the pursuit of happiness in the new homeland—The United States of America. The reader will be armed with practical knowledge on:

1. How to develop the right mindset about their wishes, their dreams, their goals, and their plans prior to making the journey

2. How to adapt in the new home - going to school, finding a job, making friends, owning a home, owning a business, owning a car, paying taxes, giving to the community and the country, and living the American Dream

You are about to embark on an incredible journey. You will learn a great deal about yourself and your new country. This process might seem mysterious, even scary at times. But the good news is that many others have gone before you, and their journey can help shine the light forward for you.

CHAPTER 2

Developing the Right Mindset

Dear brother/sister immigrant en route to the United States of America,

This chapter is the heart and the soul of this book. What I offer here will help guide you to the ultimate goal of realizing the American Dream and the pursuit of happiness. I only wish that I had such a resourceful manual back in 1969, when I was preparing to come to the USA.

Yes, I know, as the saying goes, life is about the journey, not the destination. Oh, I agree that sometimes it is better not to know until you get there...but this is your life and your family's life. You want to be as prepared for the journey as possible. Your success in your new life depends on what kind of mindset you possess prior to making the journey to the new world.

The United States of America is the most popular destination in the world. People from all over the globe dream to come to this country for the opportunity it offers. They come to participate in the American Dream and the Pursuit of Happiness.

After all these decades and many challenges, our secret sauce remains intact. We are still home to the world's finest research universities, most innovative companies, and a purely unique culture of entrepreneurship and individualism. It simply is the best country in the world for freedom of speech, entrepreneurship, and bountiful rewards for hard work.

The United States is also a complex country with many ethnic groups, political and religious views, and socioeconomic ranks. This can lead to spirited debate, as seen in the country's famously polarized politics. It can be easy to see these debates play out on television from afar and fear the country is on the brink of collapse. But in actuality, this diversity of ideas is what makes the USA the USA. With a legal status, you are free to express yourself, go anywhere, and pursue any dream you can imagine.

But please understand that it is very important you respect the people of this country and be sensitive to their way of life. You have probably been watching news about the USA. You have likely been following and engaging in gossip on social media platforms. I strongly recommend you leave all that behind and focus on being positive. Learn from the people you will meet before advancing any judgements. I recommend you focus on being creative, working hard, and giving back to your new community with no expectation of reward. You want to earn the respect of your neighbors. Being negative and critical of the American way of life will not get you many friends.

This is a country where anything is possible. Just look at all of the examples of iconic, successful companies founded and fueled by immigrants—from Google to eBay. Perhaps the most famous American entrepreneur, Apple co-founder Steve Jobs, was himself the product of Syrian immigrants. Anything you set your mind to in this country can be attained.

But in order to reach your goals, you must develop the right mindset.

It is of great importance that you read, understand, and follow the directions laid in this manual.

Regardless of your country of origin, your political and religious views, and your socioeconomic status, you will find food for thought and actionable advice here.

Take the sufficient amount of time to complete the exercises in this chapter. Ask yourself the tough questions?

1. Who are you? What are your hopes? Your dreams? Your desires?
2. What will make you happy?
3. Why the USA?
4. What do you know about the USA, its people, and culture?
5. Are you ready and willing to develop the right mindset to realize your dreams in the new homeland?

Let's look at some of these questions in greater depth and a few of your potential answers. First, I can share my own personal responses to these questions.

Who am I? Ask yourself what qualities most define what you are searching for in your new country. You might feel yourself falling into a few categories, or maybe even a combination. For me, I decided that I was a:

1. *Dreamer*
2. *Adventurer*

3. *Risk Taker*

Why America? What is attracting you to this country of all of the places in the world? Why bypass countries that may be closer in proximity?

1. The American Dream
2. New home
3. Work, house, car, family, friends

What do you know about America? Are you familiar with the basic facts and history of the place you want to call home?

1. *Facts about America*
2. *The Constitution*
3. *The People*

Developing the right mindset

We are doing this because it is very important that the mindset we develop is the *right* mindset. This will determine how easily and smoothly you will transition from your homeland to the new homeland. Let's complete the following exercises as truthfully as possible—and answer these questions for yourself.

Who am I?

1. *Dreamer*
2. *Adventurer*
3. *Risk Taker*
4. *Open Minded*

5. *Optimistic*
6. *Pessimistic*
7. *Negative*
8. *Positive*
9. *Passionate*
10. *Compassionate*
11. *Hard working*
12. *Innovative*
13. *Friendly*
14. *Entrepreneurial*
15. *Introvert*
16. *Extrovert*

Which words did you circle? Which others would you add to the list?

Why America?

1. The American Dream

Yes, we have all heard of this concept. But let's be sure to define it. Take a moment and describe to yourself what the words "American Dream" mean to you.

2. Do you plan on living permanently in the United States or just studying and working for a period of time before returning home?

3. Work, House, Car, Family, Friends - Are any of these items, in your view, part of the American Dream? Why or why not?

What I need to know

1. Facts About America

Please list five important facts about the United States; you can select from history, geography, or culture.

2. The Constitution

Please describe to yourself, in your own words, your understanding of the United States Constitution. What do you like or dislike about it? How is it still relevant to today's national climate?

3. The People

In your own words, please describe what you know about the people of the United States. What qualities distinguish them from people in other parts of the world?

***

Now that we have an idea of what you know and how you feel about the United States, the people, and the culture, let's have an open discussion and determine, based on your ideas, how you will fit in the new society. This discussion will challenge your thinking and clarify what kind of mindset you should have to live and thrive in the United States—and reach your goal of realizing your own American Dream.

I'll share with you here some general words of advice.

1. Come with an open mind. Is it not better to learn and embrace new ideas from your new countrymen and

countrywomen, instead of relying on gossip and false news and useless judgement?

2. Do not judge - not everyone is the same. Generalization is not recommended because you will end up turning off more people than you will make friends.

3. Focus on "the Immigrant Mindset" - overcome the inevitable challenges by offering solutions.

4. Be positive.

5. Be creative.

6. Give first.

7. Share your ideas without putting down the ideas of others.

8. Be respectful. Be friendly. Be open.

9. Get involved.

10. Contribute.

I have spent 48 years living in the Unites States—as a student, an employee, a tax payer, a home owner, a business owner, a husband, a father, and a neighbor. As an observer, I have learned what it takes to get respect and trust from others. I have also learned from my many mistakes and the mistakes of other immigrants. I have seen the consequences. I will share with you real stories, so you are clear on why developing the right mindset is critical to your success in reaching the American Dream.

CHAPTER 3

Setting Goals and Chasing Outcomes

In Chapter 2, we took the time to develop the right mindset. We did say over and over again how important that is for the journey. Now that you have made up your mind to make the journey to America, let's find out about how prepared you are and how much you know about the United States. Here we also show you the importance of setting goals and planning prior to traveling. Simply put, the more prepared you are, the smoother your journey will ultimately be.

Immigrants who come to America have different reasons to do so. Whatever your personal reasons, you need some resources to help you get through the first few weeks or months so that you are not left roaming the streets, looking for food and shelter.

In my case, I was very lucky. I got help with my airline ticket and had some friends to stay with when I landed in New York City on September 9, 1970. That isn't to say I did not have any challenges at all; at the time, I did not speak any English. Additionally, I did not have any money on me except for a few dollars.

I have also known other immigrants who came with nothing except the clothes they were wearing on their backs and their paperwork. A friend of mine came with a suitcase full of Moroccan bread his mother packed for him for the journey. I have also met several immigrants who were from well-to-do families in their homeland; they traveled with adequate financial resources and did not have to worry about what to do when they got to the United States.

Here is some homework for you to determine what resources are available to you and what you can do to be prepared:

1. Money

How much do you estimate you will need? Remember that major cities will require much more in the way of resources than rural communities. How much do you have? How much can you raise?

2. English Language

How well do you speak it? Write it? Read it? How and where can you learn the English prior to traveling to the United States?

3. Relationships in the United States

Do you know people living in the United States? What state? What city? Are they relatives? Are they friends? Are they willing to help you with your journey?

Whether you are traveling to study, to start a business, or to work as an employee in the United States, you need to have a clear picture of the resources available to you. They will help you transition from your homeland to the new land and reduce stress.

By now, after developing the right mindset and determining what resources you have, or should have, you should be starting to gain a good picture of what needs to be done next. Write down your goals and your plans to reach those goals. More importantly, please remember to enjoy the journey on your way to reaching the goals.

Goals

In this section, let's spend some time thinking about and writing down your goals, your dreams, your aspirations, your hopes, and your desires. I will guide you so you can develop the plans necessary to help achieve your goals.

It is critical you have a clear picture of what you are going after and how you are going to get there.

1. Why are you traveling to the United States?

Simply arriving here will be the first goal for most of us. But take time to fully consider your decision. Why the USA? Take the time to write down 3 good reasons why you decided to travel to America, as opposed to anywhere else in the world.

2. Are you coming as a student?

How long do you plan on staying as a student? Do you plan to go back home after you finish school? In my case, I was offered the opportunity to come to the United States to study medicine. My number one goal was to be enrolled in a college as a premed student and apply to medical school; my plan was to then go back home after receiving my medical degree, so I could practice medicine in Morocco.

As I will share later, my plans changed quite a bit along the way. I will cover more detail on that later, but the takeaway lesson here is to be sure to enjoy the journey while you work on achieving your goals. Sometimes other things happen, and you will find yourself pursuing other dreams and goals you did not even think about prior to traveling. More on that later.

3. Are you coming to start a business and live as a permanent resident?

This goal is certainly different from coming as a student on a temporary basis. The requirements and the resources are also different, so be clear on your intentions before you set foot on that plane or boat.

I personally know many immigrants who started small businesses and went on to become very successful. Those immigrants had their goals written and knew exactly what they wanted to do. They provided solutions to problems and developed products that people living in the United States wanted—earning significant wealth in the process.

On the flip side, I also know immigrants who started small businesses that failed for various reasons. One primary reason many fail is that they did not have goals or plans to execute. The failure rate in business in the United States is quite high compared to the success rate. Entrepreneurs who fail often go on to learn from their mistakes and try again—or they switch gears and end up looking for a job to survive.

4. Are you coming to work and live as a permanent resident? Or are you coming to work temporarily, make some money, and go back home?

***

Now that you have a clear understanding of your goals, let's move along to discussing the art of planning. Because having a good plan in place is the key to ensuring your ultimate success in America.

At this point, you have developed the right mindset and you know exactly what your goals are. Now is the time to draw plans to get you there and transition smoothly to the new life in the new homeland.

The following questions and the answers you provide will help you make the right choice and have an easy transition. The United States of America is made up of over 50 states. Each state has its own unique characteristics. If you don't have a predetermined destination for school, business, or work, there are many items you would consider in making your choice of where you want to settle.

1. Where to settle? City and state - and why?

If you have been accepted to a school or already have a job with a company, then the decision has essentially already been made. In this case, you know where you will go regardless of the items I will discuss below.

If you are still deciding on where to go to school, look for a job, or start a business, then the following list of items can help you make the decision.

   a. Existing relationships - Do you want to be near friends, relatives, or sponsors who can help you get a good start?

   b. Schools - What are you interested in studying? Every state has many universities, colleges, public and private schools, community colleges, and vocational institutions. Are you on scholarship or paying for school tuition and room and board? The cost varies significantly from school to school and state to state.

Many schools offer financial assistance to foreign students based on academics and sport scholarships.

c. There are a number of factors to consider when deciding where to start a business or look for employment:

I. Type of business or employment

II. Economic conditions

III. Cultural factors

IV. Climate conditions

There is a range of other factors to consider when deciding where to go to school, start a business, or look for a job.

2. Where to go to school and why? Don't make such a major decision based on your gut. Have you done your research?

3. Where to start a business and why?

4. Where to work and why? What attracts you to this position?

CHAPTER 4

Mastering the English Language

Congratulations on your progress so far. You have developed the right mindset, written your goals, and researched and drawn the plans for your journey to realize the American Dream. There are just a few more requirements to complete the preparation to the journey. We will explore ways to learn the English language and become familiar with different cultures. You can learn English anywhere, but to learn the American culture you will have to live it to fully appreciate it. I will guide you through the maze to make the transition smooth and successful.

This is another very important ingredient we need to add to make this a successful journey to the new homeland; without this new ingredient, it would be very challenging for you to arrive at your goal of achieving the American Dream and the pursuit of happiness. This ingredient is the secret to success in living and thriving in the United States of America. You guessed it, learning and mastering the English language.

To communicate with English-speaking people living in the United States of America is just as important, if not much more important, than developing the right mindset and setting goals.

The English language is your ticket to succeed at reaching your goals and realizing the American Dream. It is true that many immigrants who come to the United States do not speak or have a good command of the English language. They will survive, but they simply will not be very successful in moving up, going to the best schools, or getting the best jobs. It can be sad to see so many clinging only to the familiar elements of home and not fully assimilating to their new country. They are limited in their prospects to truly live the good life until they master the English language.

Whether you are coming just to visit for a short time, to study at an American college or university, to work for a company, or to start a business, you will need to communicate with others in English.

There is no shortage of opportunities to strengthen your language skills. It is true that you can learn the English language by attending special schools for non-English-speaking immigrants; it is also true that you can learn the language by informally interacting with other English-speaking people living in the area you are visiting. It will take time, and during that period, you will experience inevitable challenges. There will be painful times and frustrations when you find yourself unable to communicate and express your feelings, wishes, and desires.

I know firsthand. I have been there myself. When I came to New York on September 9, 1970, I only spoke a few words of English. I came to go to school to study medicine. I was offered a soccer scholarship at St. John Fisher College in Rochester, New York. But I was not ready to attend college because I had to learn the English language. After all, that is the language used in American colleges and universities. It would take me six months living in New York City, attending a business school with some of my Moroccan friends, and working at the New York Athletic Club at the locker room to learn English. Each day I continued to make slow and steady progress toward my ability to master the language.

During that period, I experienced so many good things, but I also suffered so many other times. When I could not understand what others were talking about, I could not fully express myself and engage in conversation with other English-speaking people. Yes, my friends spoke French and Arabic. They helped me with translations when they were with me, but when I was alone, without them, I felt lost.

I remember being envious and jealous when I saw my Moroccan friends talking in English. I still remember them laughing with other students and beautiful girls and smart teachers. I remember going to get a hot dog and a drink in the streets of New York City—but I could not do something as simple as order, because I did not know how. My friends had to order for me. I remember when I worked at the locker room of the New York Athletic Club and could not understand when club members arrived and asked for their keys, shouting key numbers for their lockers so fast. I had to remember their faces and match them with keys when I saw them coming in. Thank God for my boss, Joe, who helped me get through some challenging times.

Joe liked me because I was willing to work hard no matter what. He liked me so much that he offered me positions during the summer at the New York Athletic Club facility in Travers

Island, near New Rochelle. Joe and his brother, Tony, were very kind people.

I also learned a lot from Joe. One thing he used to say to me when I asked for a day off on Sundays was, "If you don't come Sunday, don't come Monday!" I learned very quickly that showing up to work is a serious business. People in America work hard and will respect people who do the same.

It is important that I spend time on this subject for many reasons. If you are serious about being successful in the United States, mastering the language will help you get there. Here are five major important areas in which knowing the language is critical to your success and realizing the American Dream:

1. Successful daily communication with English-speaking people living anywhere in the United States
2. Participation in social media platforms
3. Attending and succeeding in good schools
4. Finding good jobs and earning promotions
5. Planning to pursue citizenship or other goals

The next step is to show you where you can find the resources to learn English in your country of origin first. You can then continue to build your language skills both inside and outside your home when you arrive in the United States.

Maybe you are fluent in English already, or maybe you are enrolled at a school or a university in your country to learn to read, write, and speak English. If you are, I salute you and congratulate you. If you are not and you are planning to travel to the United States to study or work in the next six months, I strongly recommend that you start learning how to read, write, and speak English—sooner than later. Depending on your level of language fluency and your ability to learn it, you may expect to spend at least three to six months of studying the language to be comfortable communicating in English.

It is said that you can learn the English language anywhere, but learning the culture and the customs of the people of the United States will take longer. This guide will offer more practical tips later on how to engage with English-speaking people living in the USA. Once you are in the country, this guide will show you where to go to learn advanced English language practices.

Once you decide on the date of your travel, carve out some time between now and that date to focus intensively on your English skills. Make sure you take advantage of all the resources available to you in your country of origin to learn the English language. Trust me, you will save yourself a lot of time and a lot of frustrated moments. Once you are in the United States, you will find yourself wanting to start school or start a job or start a business right away.

There is no time to waste. I wish I'd had the wisdom and the knowledge of that before I first embarked in my journey to the United States of America. I could not enroll in college until I knew how to understand English myself.

In my case, it was a little more complicated because I was going to be enrolled as a pre-med student, which means taking science courses like biology, physics, and chemistry, along with courses like psychology, philosophy, and other electives. It was the same amount of effort as finding a part-time or a full-time job. You are required to communicate in English with your colleagues. This includes understanding when they speak, reading and writing memos, attending company meetings, writing and presenting in front of groups, and interacting with suppliers and customers, depending on what kind of work or position you are in. The same goes for starting a business: You will need the English language to understand the paperwork required to open and run a business, communicate with suppliers, and engage employees and customers.

Your mastery will also improve your social life. Improving your language skills will make it a far more enjoyable experience to watch TV, go to the movies, and get involved with your community. In every instance, you will need English to participate and enjoy the moments. If not, and if you want to continue to only communicate using your native language and hang out with your friends and relatives, you will not advance fast enough toward realizing your dreams.

Luckily, there are a variety of resources in your home country. When you arrive in the United States, you can learn and master the basics of the English language even easier. I will mention some of the most popular resources worth considering. Let's take a look at what you have available in your home country prior to your journey:

1. If you have the budget, enroll in a language school that teaches conversational English. This will allow you to communicate with your teachers and fellow students in English only. It will accelerate your learning of the language so you can hit the ground running from day one.

2. Check with the American embassy or consulate in your city and inquire about the availability of free classes for people traveling to the United States to study or work or start a business.
3. Find English courses online and enroll in one or two classes. Remember that you will need a good device and a good internet connection to enjoy the experience.
4. Sign up for a free Facebook account and other social media platforms. Join different groups in which members communicate in English and build relationships.
5. Challenge yourself to read books, newspapers, magazines, and articles written in English.
6. Watch American TV shows and movies.
7. Listen to American Radio shows and songs.
8. Practice writing to and speaking with English-speaking people in your city or country.
9. Visit American public libraries.
10. Read about the American constitution, history, culture, and customs.

If you follow the step-by-step recommendations listed so far in this book, you will be prepared and ready to make the journey toward the new land for a new life and experience. The learning continues when you arrive at the United States. Remember the mindset, the goals, and the plans you worked on. Remember what you are here for.

Always remember to be excited, full of enthusiasm, and bring a positive perspective, even during the challenging times. Listen and learn from everyone you come in contact with.

Be outgoing, don't be shy. You will make mistakes at times, but that's okay. It is a universal part of the immigrant experience to feel like an outsider at one point or another. We have all experienced it, and we all overcome it. I urge you to remember that the majority of American people are good people—very hospitable, understanding, and compassionate. If you show that you are a good person that is willing to learn, work hard, and improve your life and your family's life, you will be welcomed. If you are willing to share your culture and your wisdom, you will get the respect of your new neighbors and will be welcomed with warmth.

I remember the first time I met families in Rochester, New York, through Monsignor Kaiser of Catholic Relief Services. I was afforded so many opportunities to get to know Americans on a personal basis. I attended their Christmas parties, watched football games in their living rooms, and attended picnics and other events with them. To me, they have always been very hospitable. Even when I was still new to the language and could command relatively few words, they always said, "Your English is wonderful." I will always remember that. It shows that they were very understanding of my situation and were willing to say a few words of encouragement to make me feel as though I belonged.

After 48 years living in the United States of America—as a student, an employee, a tax payer, a home owner, a car owner, a business owner, a husband, and a father—I still learn English and still make mistakes. That is okay. None of us will ever achieve perfect mastery (perhaps even in our native tongue). But I am very comfortable now understanding many topics in English and communicating with many English-speaking people in a variety of circumstances. I enjoy the experience, and maybe it is a part of the American Dream to find myself in this situation. I remain confident and always willing to help, discover, and learn. I will share more with you in the next few pages.

I encourage you to use your time wisely because time is precious. As they say in the United States, or anywhere in the world, time is money. Let us discover together the many circumstances where you can learn more English, whether you are at home, school, work, or in the neighborhood.

1. When you are at home, you may be surrounded by many tools and devices that will allow you to learn many things in English and master the language. Don't think of these gadgets as merely entertaining diversions; think of them as educational tools. Watch the news and educational shows on TV. Surf the internet to read and learn about topics for your studies, your work, or just general topics for learning purposes. You may be living with roommates or have a family, with a spouse and children. I encourage you to speak English as much as you can because it will help you get closer to your goals and dreams.

Resist the temptations to speak your native language; instead, watch shows, read books, articles, and magazines in English, and not listen to songs from your native country. There is nothing wrong about feeling homesick. It happens to all of us, and you will be homesick at one time or another. There is nothing wrong with wanting to speak your native language with friends and relatives. There is nothing wrong with teaching your kids or spouse or others to speak your native language. The important thing is to take advantage of every opportunity to master the English language. You will find more joy when you understand what people are talking about...whether you are watching a sporting event or talk show on TV or reading a newspaper or magazine written in English.

2. When you are at school, at work, or interacting on social media, always communicate in English. Listen and learn from others: your teachers, your coworkers, your employees. When engaging friends on social media—such as Facebook, Twitter, Instagram, LinkedIn, and others—write in English, express yourself in English, and remember to be courteous and respectful of others.

Again, resist the temptations to engage friends on social media using your native language. There is nothing wrong with that, except that you have a limited amount of time. You want to be wise about mastering the English language.

3. When you are out and about in the community or traveling within the United States, I encourage you to communicate in English. Whether you are talking to neighbors, shopping at the grocery stores, going to sporting events, or dropping your kids at school, speak in English. Anywhere you come in contact with people, use the English language to communicate.

You will find a number of references, websites, and places where you can find many resources available to further your learning of the English Language. One such a reference online is a welcoming guide for new immigrants, "Welcome to the

United States: A Guide For New Immigrants" https://www.uscis.gov/sites/default/files/files/nativedocuments/M-617.pdf. Go to public libraries and ask the librarian to help you find books and audio cassettes for learning English as a second language.

Learning to communicate using the English language will open so many doors that will lead you closer to the American Dream and the pursuit of happiness. In chapter 5, I will discuss the importance of keeping an open mind in your new homeland.

CHAPTER 5

The Innocence of Youth
(Learn like a baby ... absorb like a sponge)

Resist the temptation to pre-judge your new home. Instead, give people the benefit of the doubt—after all, the majority of people in the United States are good people. The more open-minded you are, the more opportunity you have to interact with neighbors and community members. Have empathy. Learn from everyone and share your culture with all.

As I mentioned earlier in this book, the United States of America is made up of many different states, different ethnic groups, different religious tendencies, different socioeconomic classes, and at least two major political parties. It may appear at times that there is division among different groups of Americans based on the diversity that exists. In some ways, it is natural for a country that is home to people from just about every country on the planet to have some differences when we all come together.

On the other hand, Americans are united under so much—the flag of the United States, the constitution, the English language, the principles of democracy and freedom of Speech, due process, liberty and justice for all. I am sure that many people around the globe are following what is happening in this country socially, economically, and politically. I am sure that there are many opinions—good, bad, or indifferent—about the country and its people. Suffice it to say, no country is entirely immune to society and life challenges. Every nation has its own share of problems, challenges, and blessings.

It is possible that you also have been following what is going on in the United States by watching the news or following gossip through social media and you have your own opinions.

For your own success in living and thriving in the United States, it is very important that you stay focused on your ultimate goal of realizing the American Dream....because the American Dream is alive and well, regardless of what some people may be saying or thinking. The beauty of being in this country is that you are free to express your opinions. Freedom of speech is such a powerful concept. But before you speak, please think and ask yourself the following questions:

1. Do I know enough about the culture and the customs of the people living in the United States at this point to offer my own opinion?

2. Do I want to make friends and acquaintances and build solid relationships to help me move forward with my progress and my journey toward my American Dream? Or do I want to irritate people with my judgement of others and my criticism of the way of life here? Who am I to judge?

I submit to you that it is advisable you focus on the things that will help you reach your goals and realize your dreams. This chapter will guide you and offer a step-by-step approach on where to focus your time and energy and how to become better on a day-to-day basis.

Put yourself in a state of mind and think back to when you were growing up—you were learning and absorbing new things, just like a baby growing up. When you reflect back on this time, you will recall the innocence of youth. You will recall how you were open to learning new things and getting better.

In this chapter, you will be exposed to three areas of focus:

1. Keep an open mind - I will show you how and why.

2. Learn from others. I will share with you things I learned by listening and learning.

3. Learn to give and share.

Keep an open mind about people, their culture, and living amongst them.

Here is an easy way for you to look at this—people are people everywhere, with different looks and different behaviors and different customs and different beliefs. The same goes in your country when you go from city to city. You will find people who may speak the same language but have different ways of looking at life, thinking, and living. To know more about them, you will need to interact, be respectful, listen, and understand their ways before they can understand yours.

It is the same way when you arrive in the United States. People are people, regardless of their ethnic background or religious or political beliefs. They go to work to provide for their families, go to schools to learn, laugh, cry, travel, celebrate holidays and sports, eat, drink, sleep, and exercise. Some get involved in politics…some don't. To understand how people live and why they do certain things and behave in certain ways in society, you will need to know a little more about where they come from, their heritage, and their history.

Let me illustrate this using my experience and my first impressions when I landed in New York City in September 1970. Sure, certain things were different than they are now, but many things also remain the same about people, their culture, and their customs. My goal was to attend school, and I needed to learn English as fast I could. The so-called Big Apple could be quite intimidating for a young 20-year-old from Morocco. The buildings, the subways, the people, the lights, Times Square, Broadway—there were so many great things about the city that made you believe you died and went to a different universe all together.

But when you open your eyes and walk in the streets or ride the subways, you start embracing the realities of a big city—a melting pot. There are all kinds of people, from all walks of life, working and living in New York and the surrounding boroughs like Brooklyn, Queens, the Bronx, and Staten Island, as well as the neighboring states of New Jersey and Connecticut.

There are tourists from all over the world visiting different landmarks, such as the Statue of Liberty, The Empire State Building, Times Square, and many museums and other places in the city. People are eating in coffee shops and restaurants, riding buses, taxis, and subways. I was quickly reminded of the movie *West Side Story*…and I was now in the middle of it all. Yes, you can learn a lot just being in this beautiful yet mysterious city. To learn about the people living in New York City, about their cultures and their customs, and about how to live here, I realized I needed to keep an open mind. I needed to view the world just like a baby—absorbing things that would help me in my journey to realizing my American dream.

Yes, the world was mine now. There was so much I could learn by just watching, listening, and interacting with people.... and I was only there for 48 hours, and in one part of a big city. Imagine all of the other cities in the state of New York, and across many more states in the USA. There was so much to learn—and I was ready to keep an open mind.

In my small world, in the beginning, I learned from my interactions with people on a day-to-day basis, being in school and at work, and by learning to survive and thrive. I found that another excellent way of learning is to be able to share and give to others.

To keep an open mind is to let yourself learn from others and your surroundings. One thing to keep in mind is that you want to learn the good stuff. Have you ever heard the expression, "Garbage in, garbage out?" What you really want is the good stuff. To get the good stuff, you need to be with the right people and in the right places. Stay focused on your goals. Don't be distracted by things that are not going to help you with your goals. In a big city like New York, there are many good people, many good places, and many good things to do, but there are also many temptations that can ultimately lead to one's destruction. Embrace the former and avoid the latter.

Learn from others: how to communicate, what to learn in school and at work, and how to thrive and survive.

When you are alone and homesick, there is a tendency to compensate by either being with good people or bad people.

It is true that you can be with both. I prefer to be with good people, and I am not judging the other people. Good people tend to be stable, focused on the good stuff, and have good communication skills. They use the right language and behave like normal people do. Trust me—these are the people you want to be around and learn from.

The other kind of people, the ones you want to avoid being around, tend to be erratic. They don't have focus on what is good for them and their communication skills are often lacking. If your goal is to learn how to speak proper English, how to express yourself clearly, and how to stay healthy physically and mentally, then you want to be with good people.

They can come from all walks of life. They don't have to be rich or poor. They don't have to be beautiful or not beautiful. They don't have to be black or white or any other color. They don't have to be Democrat, Republican, or Independent; they don't have to be Catholic, Protestant, Jewish, Muslim, or any other religion. There are good and bad people in any of the categories mentioned. If your goal is to become a better communicator, then you want to be around good people who have control of themselves, the language they use, and the behavior they exhibit.

Even in the streets of big cities, you will find good people, but you also can encounter some other kinds—people who use foul language, abuse alcohol, use drugs, and commit other sins. You want to avoid the latter.

Schools and work places tend to have a "safer environment," but even here you are going to experience running into good students or not so good students. You will encounter great coworkers and subordinates or not so good coworkers and subordinates. You will have to make the choice with whom you want to associate and learn from.

At school, I experienced firsthand the major differences that come from being with serious students and learned a lot from them on how they behave and succeed. I also experienced being around the other kind of students—the ones who like to party more than study. The ones who very rarely succeed. I submit that if I had to do it all over again, I would spend my precious time with the serious crowd...the ones who want to help you do better in school and other school activities. Being with the other crowd has a higher probability of leading you in the wrong direction...drinking, smoking, and other unhealthy behaviors. In schools, teachers, schoolmates, and other educators are watching how people behave in the classrooms and outside the classrooms. Some of these folks write recommendations when you are ready to apply to medical or dental or law schools. You want them to know the good things about you.

At work, you want to focus on doing the best job possible and get it done under deadline. At the workplace, you will find coworkers who just like to gossip and spend hours talking about others, not accomplishing the work they are getting paid for. You will find jealous coworkers who may cause you troubles.

But there are also many coworkers who appreciate having a job and want to keep it to support themselves and their families. Just like schools, at work you have coworkers, supervisors, and managers watching everyone's work ethics, performances, and behaviors. These managers decide on your merit pay increase and your advancement within the organization. You never want to give your boss a reason not to like or promote you or give you a salary increase. Don't give them a reason to hesitate about writing a good recommendation letter when you need it.

In the workplace, you want to be positive, creative, helpful, a team player, enthusiastic, and always on time for work, for a meeting, or for a presentation. You want to leave good impressions all day, every time.

Whether you are in school, at work, at home, at a restaurant, at a mall, riding a bus or the subway, at a party, in a park, or just walking to school or work, you have the opportunity to interact with people, communicate, and exhibit your best behavior or your worst. It is always best to exhibit your best self. It goes a long way. Bad behavior may impress some at times, but you don't need recognition from that crowd. Focus on the stuff that will make you better every day and get you closer to your goals.

This is how you learn to survive and thrive in a new environment with strangers. Some of them will be your best friends and will cheer you on. They will help realize the American Dream of yours and the Pursuit of Happiness. Once again, by reading this book, you are receiving the best advice from a man with experience in both the good and the not-so-good worlds of the USA. I wish I had a manual such as this before I took my journey. I am thrilled that I can share this with you so you are prepared in making your journey to America.

Another part of keeping an open mind and learning is opening yourself up to others and sharing your experiences, talents, and resources. In the next few pages, I will share with you how to learn, to give, and to share your time, your money, and your talents with the community and the country. It is by helping others that you get much in return.

Learn to give and share time, money, and talents with the community and the country

By keeping an open mind and learning from others, you will find yourself beginning to understand the new environment and the new culture and customs of the people around you. It is a wonderful experience—if you embrace it, you will enjoy it and make plenty of progress toward your goal of reaching the American Dream. One way of accelerating the process is to jump right in and start living as though you are a native—as though you really belong. Start meeting and impressing people. Start making friends and acquaintances who will be there to help you and support you as you move closer to your goal.

We all possess certain things we can share with others—time, money, and talents. Whether you are enrolled in schools, working at a job, or running a business, the gift of sharing and giving will place you in a higher position when you participate and give of yourself to others. You have probably often heard people talk about this: "Give and you shall receive." "Help others get what they want so you get what you want."

You may find yourself saying, "I don't have time. I don't have money to give away, and I certainly don't have any talents to share with others."

No worries—this manual will show you how you discover what you have and how to use it in this context of giving and sharing so you can receive back from others. Let's take a look at each of the three elements, one at a time.

1. Time

Regardless of how much time we think we all have, there are only so many hours in the day, so many days in the week, and so many weeks in the year. We all have the same amount of time. Here is the secret to success: where you spend your limited amount of time and how effective you are in planning to spend it will dictate what kind of results you will get. What activities are you involved with when you are not studying, working, or running your business?

Some people complain that they never have enough time to do anything beyond studying, going to work, or running a business. Yet they seem to find time to do many useless and unproductive activities. As immigrants, we have tendencies to want to hang around people who speak our native language, eat our native food, and listen to our native songs. Some of us waste time doing nothing but eating, drinking, and having parties. There is nothing wrong with having a little bit of fun to relax and recharge, either after school and working hours or during the weekends and holidays.

But I argue there is something wrong if we spend the majority of our time doing essentially nothing but partying. Let me illustrate this by going back to my early days in New York City and when I attended college. I had friends from Morocco, and we used to spend free time together, mostly during weekends and holidays. We used to cook Moroccan food, organize parties, invite other Moroccan friends, communicate with each other in our native language, and listen to Moroccan songs. Sometimes we had non-Moroccan guests, and that was just about the only time we exchanged a few words with them in English, if they only spoke that language.

Again, there is nothing wrong having some fun once in a while…but when it becomes a habit, doing the same thing every weekend and every holiday, it can be a trap of sorts. When I look back, I realize how much time I wasted instead of being somewhere else, learning the English language. I could have been going to the library, for instance. I could have been visiting museums and monuments, learning the history of the United States. I could have been finding another part-time job to help me save money for my school and my trips back to Morocco. I realized that I spent so many hours doing nothing constructive that was going to help me get better with my language, my assimilation, and my fast transition to the life in the United States. My time in college illustrates this even better.

In January 1970, I enrolled in St. John Fisher College in Rochester, New York. My English was a little bit better, but it still needed a lot of improvement. That winter was a brutal one. There was so much snow that year—so high that some college roommates, classmates, and I used to jump from the roof of the dormitory into the piles of snow. I enrolled as a pre-med student, which meant a lot of studying biology, chemistry, physics, math, and some elective courses like psychology and philosophy. I was also on a soccer scholarship, which meant practice during the week and games at home and away on Saturdays.

I took a part-time job at the cafeteria and another part-time job at the campus club at night serving drinks. In addition, I worked at a nice restaurant, The Maple Wood Inn Restaurant, as a busboy. Suffice it to say, I was quite a busy bee on campus. Then, on some nights and weekends, some of my friends and I used to hang around a pub called Checkos. This was the hottest gathering place in town for the all-male students from St. John

Fisher College to get together with the many beautiful girls from Nazareth College.

While I spent a lot of time having fun and partying, my serious pre-med roommates were typically at the library or in their rooms studying. They were getting ready for quizzes, tests, and exams. Some of them went on to become doctors and dentists.

Yes, I had plenty of extra time. I regret only spending part of it doing something constructive, like going to the library and being with the serious students who spent a majority of their time studying and learning. Yes, I was a good student, but I needed to be much better to compete as a pre-med student.

I learned a lot about the value of time. I enjoyed many aspects of sharing time and moments with other college friends and girlfriends. I used and gave of my time to earn extra pocket money. I received some value by giving and sharing my time. I was among English-speaking college friends, so I had no choice but to communicate in English. In order to simply find a date and be with the date, I had to communicate in English and give some of my time to be with them.

I really enjoyed my three years in college—I played soccer, made many friends, and practically always had a smile on my face. I worked and made extra money during the school year and in the summer. I attended concerts and college sport events. I had dates and girlfriends. As I spoke French, I was the president of the French Club for both St. John Fisher and Nazareth College, which meant some fun trips to Quebec and parties organized by the club. But I needed to spend more time on things related to medical schools. I will cover more later on about volunteering your time to give back to the community and the country.

2. Money

There are a number of ways you can think about sharing and giving when it comes to money. Whether you are student in school, working full-time or part-time, running a business, or just visiting for a short period as a tourist, you will need money to survive. Whether it is money you brought with you from home to use until you get a job or money you get by working part-time or full-time, you will use it for necessities. Everything in the United States costs money. There is no way around it. If you are not enrolled in a government program that helps you with rent, groceries, or other expenses, you will need money for the items listed below. This is one way you will be sharing, giving, or using money to help businesses and other entities that provide goods and services.

Keep in mind a few of the most important expenses you will need to budget for.

a. Where you live - room and board in schools, renting, leasing, buying property, obtaining mortgage, staying in hotel/motels, etc.

b. Food and beverage - Groceries, eating out.

c. Insurance - Home/rent, medical, car, dental, vision.

e. Transportation - Car, motorcycle/bicycle, bus, subway, taxis.

f. Clothes/shoes

g. Taxes

h. Miscellaneous

All of these costs have a way of compounding and spiraling. Err on the side of caution and save more than you think you need to budget. You will thank yourself later on.

3. Talents

We all possess talents and gifts we can share with others. If we can't give time or money, there are many skills, talents, and other gifts we can share with the community and the country to make this a better world. In the next chapter, we will discuss in detail how we can give our time, energy, and skills to give back to the community and the country. Remember—the more you give, the more you receive, and the more you assimilate and adapt in the new homeland.

- a. Volunteering - This is an area of enormous opportunity for assimilation in which you can get involved with schools, charities, work, churches, hospitals, and nursing homes.

- b. Sports - This is another major area where you can play a major role as a coach and a mentor to the next generation.

- c. Community/Country - If you offer your time, your money, and your skills to the community and the country, you will find yourself with much deeper relationships in your community—whether you teach others a different language, instruct a student in how to play an instrument, or serve in some capacity with different groups and nonprofit organizations.

Again, to be accepted in any community, you want to engage and get involved. The sooner, the better, so you can quickly adapt and make a smooth transition to start living your dream in the United States.

In the next chapter, you will find many examples where you can give of your time and share your skills and talents. Stay excited, positive, and full of enthusiasm. Learn from others. Sometimes a friendly smile, a helping hand, and a good attitude can go a long way.

CHAPTER 6

Be Ready to Give More

You have probably heard people say, "The more you give, the more you receive." If you follow the art of "selling" principles, you will hear coaches and mentors talk about the concept of helping others get what they want so you get what you want. In order to adapt and assimilate yourself in this new world—you want to be ready to give more of yourself. Writing this guide for you is my way of giving back to the community, the country, and the world.

I am fulfilling one of my passions, goals, and purposes in life—helping others succeed in life and business. In this case, my intention is to help you reach the American Dream and the Pursuit of Happiness in the United States. I want you to do great and achieve your goals. I want you and your family to succeed in the United States, to enjoy what this beautiful country has to offer. I want you to taste the American Dream, embrace it, and live it.

You may ask, "What exactly can I do to help others in my new community? How?"

I am glad you asked that question, because in the United States, people who love and cherish this land want to make it a better place for those to follow—their children and grandchildren and the many generations to come.

Even in this richest country in the world, there are many people who need assistance with a variety of things to carry on with their lives. Even in this country with so much beauty and wealth, there is not enough money, not enough man power, and not enough resources to go around for all of the states, the cities, and the small communities.

So, there is a great need for assistance from all of us living in the country who want to help many causes without getting paid. This country greatly respects people who serve, defend, and protect—think of people in the military, the police, the firefighters, the volunteers for nonprofit organizations, and many others who help with the young, the elderly, the poor, and the sick. These people are respected and cherished because they give of their lives, their time, their money, their compassion, and their passion. They are revered in society and they stand out. They are recognized, and they are rewarded. To help you discover what is out there and how you can join and stand out in your community, I will focus on three different areas in particular.

1. Volunteering - in schools/charity organizations, churches and other religious centers, hospitals and nursing homes, the fire department. You can give of your time, money, and skills.

2. Sports - There are so many different sports of widespread popularity in the United States - baseball, football, basketball, soccer, tennis, golf, swimming, volleyball, and

many more. You can give of your time and your skills as a coach, a player, a manager, or an aid to managers.

3. Community and country - Vote when you are eligible. Become a member of a school board, run for office in your city or town or state, or join a local civic organization.

Volunteering

What is beautiful about volunteering is that you get to choose when to volunteer based on the extra free time you have available. You get to decide your cause based on your passion, your skills, and your ability to help others in need in that area. By volunteering in your community, you will meet many people with the same passion. You also will make friends, and you may even find the love of your life, if you are lucky.

Schools

Because of budgetary limitations, schools depend on parents and others in the community to help. For example, when we lived in Cheshire, Connecticut, my wife, Connie, volunteered as a substitute teacher in our local elementary schools. Full-time teachers do get sick once in a while or have civic duties they have to attend to, so substitute teachers are called to help by watching and helping students read, write, or do homework. My wife made friends, and my two daughters were always happy to see her in school. Contrary to the popular myth of kids being embarrassed to be seen with their parents in public, they were very proud of her volunteering. I have also seen many parents and others in the community volunteer as librarians and traffic control agents. I have seen parents help in the cafeteria during lunch hours. There is simply no shortage of ways to get involved and make your local school an even better place.

Charity Organizations

There is a multitude of nonprofit organizations in need of your time and presence, both in the day-to-day operations of their organizations and when they have special events. Their mission is to raise money to help with causes. You can find many nonprofit organizations in your community that you can join based on your passion and your interests in the cause. Here, again, you will meet many other volunteers and develop healthy relationships, which will help you with your goals of becoming a good citizen and realizing your dreams.

Churches and Religious Centers

Based on your faith and beliefs, you will find many churches and religious institutions where you can become a practicing member, a volunteer, or both. These places are well-known for greeting newcomers with wide open arms. These religious centers often get involved with helping the poor and the homeless by providing food, clothing, and shelter, and even assisting with locating jobs for those in need of work.

Hospitals and Nursing Homes

Helping the sick and the elderly is one of the most popular areas in which you can really help and make a difference. Again because of budgetary limitations, hospitals and nursing homes depend on volunteers to assist with non-nursing and physician functions. For example, you might help at the information desks when patients and visitors arrive. Or you might help with serving meals to patients. Here, again, you have the opportunity to meet people and make new friends who can help you toward realizing your dreams. People know people, and they can introduce you to other people who may be in a position to help you get a job, start a business, or attend a good school.

Fire Departments and Police Departments

This area of volunteering is enormously popular because people involved in these departments save lives and property. These departments also have their own associations and charities you can join.

***

As you can see, there is no lack of opportunities to volunteer. There is need all around us. It is up to you to look around, find what interests you, and identify what will help you build healthy relationships in your community and advance your stepping stones toward your goal of realizing your American Dream.

In the next few pages, I will help you discover opportunities to get involved with sports, as a coach or a team player, and how to make so many friends in this area. By giving before receiving and helping others get what they want, you will also move closer to attaining your own goals in life.

All About Sports

I am writing this in March 2018. It is a busy time for sports—right now the NBA Basketball season is underway with March Madness and the Final Four. Golf is in full swing. Baseball training camps are open, and the football season just concluded with the Super Bowl in February. Of course, the soccer season is still ongoing as well. Simply put, there are teams and fans for almost every sport in the USA.

Welcome to the ultimate sporting experience in the whole world. You don't want to miss out on this—talking sports and asking about the weather are the most common topics people in the United States engage in when not talking politics or economics.

When you follow sports in the USA, you learn about teams and players. You learn about schools and cities and states and fans. You learn about how much money professional athletes make. There are so many sports in all states. States, cities, and schools are well known for their teams and fans. Getting involved in sports as a fan, a player, a coach, a marketer, or a helper in any position is an opportunity for you to learn the American culture. It is an opportunity for you to share your athletic skills, as well as maybe your managerial and coaching talents. It is an opportunity for you to live and enjoy the experience with your friends, neighbors, and others in the community.

It you can't attend live sporting events in person, the majority of sports are shown on television in homes, sport bars, hotels, and airports—practically everywhere. No matter where you go, you will find a TV blaring away with the big game—and a friendly fan on the next stool over to join you in cheering on your team.

To give you a primer for what to expect, here is a list of major sports dominating this sector and some of the well-known teams and players in the USA. (The team and player ranking will change over time, of course, based on their performance.)

Professional and College Sports

- Baseball (Astros, Dodgers, Yankees, Red Sox)
- Football (Patriots, Cowboys, Saints, Steelers)
- Basketball (Golden State Warriors, Cavaliers)
- Volleyball
- Soccer
- Hockey
- Swimming
- Track & Field
- Cycling
- Golf
- Tennis
- Lacrosse
- Boxing
- Wrestling
- Table Tennis
- Archery
- Boating
- Gymnastics
- Winter Sports and Summer Sports

Think Olympics and Championships

***

The sport sector employs millions upon millions of people. It represents one of the fundamental tenets of American life. The faster you learn about things like sports, the faster you will assimilate in this society.

Families and their children get involved in sports at an early age. This is where you may have the ultimate opportunity to give to the community as a coach, a player, or a manager.

Giving Back to Community and Country

People from all over the globe migrate to the United States for many reasons—fleeing religious or political prosecution, seeking freedom, pursuing higher education, or simply striving for a better job and better lifestyle.

There is one main reason that seems to be true for all immigrants—the Opportunity to realize the American Dream and the Pursuit of Happiness.

We all define it differently. Many of us might consider it to follow a series of well-trod steps: get a degree from a good school, find a good job, start a successful business, buy a home, buy a car, and start a family—and even pay taxes!

There are many people who come to the United States to visit as tourists, to study, to find a job, or to start a business. Many fall in love with this beautiful homeland, its people, and their way of life. They are so fond of the country that they decide to stay, become US citizens, and start a family. Many decide to give back of their time, their money, and their skills and talents. They develop successful companies with innovative solutions to solve problems. Many residents and their children even go on to serve in the military or run for political office and help in bringing about positive change. Those are examples of the ultimate giving back to the community and the country.

Some other example of high achievement to consider:

1. Teaching - there are numerous examples of immigrants who came to the states and became great teachers of various scientific disciplines—physics, chemistry, genetics, music, and dance. Immigrants have gone on to serve as great coaches and athletes in gymnastics, soccer, baseball, basketball, and other sports.

2. Sharing your innovation and novel ideas - there are many immigrants who came here to study or to start a business. There is not enough space here to fully recount the many examples of how many immigrants are heading successful high-tech companies because of their genius and innovation. They do include some of the most iconic and successful tech brands in the world, such as Apple, Google, eBay, and PayPal, to name a few.

3. Serving - those immigrants who go on to become permanent residents and citizens offer the greatest examples of giving back to the community and the country, and even the world. Some join the military and give their lives to protect the nation. Others become involved in politics and run for office in their towns and cities; some even go on to run as U.S. senators and U.S. representatives to legislate and balance power from the executive and the judicial branches.

You have gained a good idea of what kind of mindset you possess and what your goals and plans are. You've learned the importance of the English language and keeping an open mind. And, finally, you understand how you can give back to the community and country so you can assimilate and start living your American Dream.

This guide has provided what you need to begin living in the United States one day at a time and how you can begin to chase the goals you have written down back in Chapter 3. It is time that you go to work and live your American Dream. In Chapters 7 and 8, we will discover what it will take for you and your loved ones to be happy—and we will review some ways to be successful in reaching the happiness.

Chapter 9 will review what your day-to-day life might look like in the new homeland. You have sacrificed a lot—now it is time to enjoy the fruit of your labor. Now is the time to start tasting the American Dream and build on it for the ultimate pursuit of happiness.

CHAPTER 7

Recap: The American Dream for Immigrant Entrepreneurs

Part I

Wherever you are in this world, close your eyes and dream of one place you would rather be that will make you happy right now. Let your mind run wild, no matter how impossible it might seem to accomplish the vision in your mind right now.

You might imagine places like New York City, Manhattan, Los Angeles, or San Francisco. You might envision Dallas, Austin, Orlando, Miami, Honolulu, or Maui. Your thoughts might drift to Chicago, Atlanta, Seattle, or Boston. You might let your thoughts drift to the national capitol of Washington, D.C.

If you have seen those places in your mind, you are dreaming about a country called the United States of America. It is a place where real dreams come true—as hokey as it might sound, it is very much true. I am living here now and have been here since 1970. I have seen enormous change in that time, and I would not have traded this experience for anything in the world. I want to help you get here too, to realize your American Dream. I want to help you get here, prepared and ready to live the life you dreamt about and the happiness that comes with it.

I want to make your transition from your homeland to the new land very smooth, so you can assimilate and adapt very quickly in the USA. To accomplish this and enjoy the journey as you go, it was important to discuss the Idea of the American Dream and make it a reality, not just a concept. In Chapter 1, I wanted you to dream it, feel it, taste it, and live it. In Chapter 2, I helped you develop the right mindset needed to make your journey enjoyable. In Chapter 3, you learned about setting goals and writing down elaborate plans to accomplish those precious goals. In Chapter 4, you learned how important the English language is for your survival and success among English-speaking people in the USA.

In Chapter 5, you learned the importance of keeping an open mind and learning from others, so you can succeed in the new homeland. In Chapter 6, you became familiar with the concepts and the realities of giving of yourself to the community and the country you are about to visit.

Now you are ready for the journey. You have packed and have your passport in your hand. Say goodbye to family and friends and the homeland—and begin the road to the American Dream. God is with you. Have no fear. Take this book with you and read it when you are alone or homesick…it will remind you about why you are here right now and why you are going through with this journey.

You have arrived at your destination. Now what? Well, you will take it one day at a time. And don't forget to enjoy each step of the journey.

One Day at a Time

What is the best way to find happiness in your new home? You can attain it by believing in yourself and by fully embracing the goals you chase. The more passionate and enthusiastic you grow about your new home, the quicker you will adapt and find and make new friends.

This chapter will guide you through the day by day living and accomplishing what you came here for...the American Dream.

1. Always remember your "WHY" you came here...believe in yourself, embrace the change, and chase your goals.

2. Be passionate, get excited, be enthusiastic, and stay positive.

3. Start living the Dream...at school, at work. Embrace each milestone along the course of your journey—your first home, your first car, your new friends, your new family.

Why you came. You came from a faraway land to realize that dream of yours. Partake in the American Dream. You are here, and no matter what happens, you need to believe in yourself and what you can accomplish. Embrace the change in your life, don't run away from it, and don't hide from it. This is your opportunity to get closer to your dream. Review the written goals and the plans you have committed to paper—in fact, I recommend you carry them with you everywhere you go so that they will always be on your mind. Look at them every morning when you get up and review them every night before you go to sleep. Monitor your progress and see how you are doing with your goals—be honest with yourself and don't traffic in happy falsehoods. Chase your goals. If you need to change a few things to help you get your goals accomplished faster and better, don't hesitate. This is how you learn. You will inevitably make some mistakes along the way—learn from them. You will fall down once in a while, and you just have to get up and try again. Remember, you will be among many good people...show them respect, smile, and always be ready to help. They will help you and take care of you, just like many took care of me. Enjoy your way to the top.

Part II - Get excited

Be passionate, be enthusiastic, and stay positive

Excitement is contagious.

When you show excitement about an opportunity or passion for a cause, others can feel that same energy. When you are enthusiastic at school and at work, when you are always positive, you are showing the world who you are. That is why a smile on your face is always your best bet if you can't say something impressive right away.

How you shake hands with people is also another way of communication. Depending on whether you are shaking hands with a man or a woman, the pressure and the grip will be different. You would be amazed at how large an impression you can make with something as small as the right handshake.

Whether you are at work, in school, running a business, playing a game, or participating in a company meeting, get excited and show your involvement with any project or event. People around you will notice that passion. Your attitude and your excitement will motivate them to interact with you, befriend you, and ultimately help you.

What is passion?

Passion is when you put more energy into something than is required to do it. Hard work is not nearly as arduous if you spend it directing your energies toward something that you genuinely enjoy and find success in. So be passionate about what you spend your time doing. You will invariably go much farther than you ever could by working hard in a subject that repels or bores you.

What is enthusiasm?

We can define this quality as intense and eager enjoyment and interest. Your enthusiasm about a project, an event, or any function will show in your eyes, in your face, and all over your body. Always show enthusiasm, and success will follow.

What does being positive mean?

It means looking toward the good things of life. An example of being positive is to have a good attitude; an example of someone positive is a motivational speaker. Have you ever heard a speaker who so roused your excitement and sense of passion that you couldn't wait to leave the room and get to work? It is incredible how motivating the right positive outlook can be.

You want to stay positive all the time, and don't let anyone who thinks negatively invade your space. Guard your thoughts carefully; life is too short to bother with negative energy. Do not associate with negative people. Be around positive and optimistic people who always look toward the good things in life.

Part III - Living the Dream

What is the "American Dream"?

By now, we have revised some definitions of the American Dream, but your conception may continue to change the more you learn and reflect on the realities of coming to your new home. I selected a few definitions that I like, which resonate especially well with me.

> A. *"The ideal that every U.S. citizen should have an equal opportunity to achieve success and prosperity through hard work, determination, and initiative."*
>
> B. *"Success= the accomplishment of an aim or purpose."*

"Prosperity is the state of flourishing, good fortune or successful social status. Prosperity often encompasses wealth but also includes other factors which can be independent of wealth to varying degrees, such as happiness and health."

I like this definition because it focuses on hard work and determination. To realize the American Dream, you need determination and you need to put in the work. Make sure you review the definitions below of the words used—hard work, determination, and initiative.

- *Hard Work = A great deal of effort or endurance*
- *Determination = Firmness of purpose; Resoluteness*
- *Initiative = Ability to assess and initiate things independently*

> B. *The American Dream is the belief that anyone, regardless of where they were born or what class they were born into, can attain their own version of success in a society where*

upward mobility is possible for everyone. The American Dream is achieved through sacrifice, risk-taking, and hard work, not by chance.

I like this definition because it spells out the fact that anyone can attain their own version of success in the society they live in, regardless of where they were born or what class they were born into. This is one of the main reasons many people from all over the globe come to the United States of America in search of this opportunity.

C. *A concept which includes the opportunity for freedom, wealth, and prosperity in the U.S.*

I like this definition because of the emphasis on Freedom and prosperity.

An example of the American Dream is when you come to America, build a business, and become successful. Another is when you are doing better than your parents, owning your own home, and being financially free.

Based on the many definitions and meanings of the American Dream, suffice it to say that not everybody will experience the same American Dream. Some may be content with getting a good job with a good company, buying a house and a car, and helping their kids go to school; others may consider The American Dream based on the size of their bank accounts, real estate portfolio, and other materialistic things.

Others may be happy and claim they have reached the American Dream if they build a successful business that allows them to live comfortably.

One common theme among all these different scenarios is that people are happy and financially free. They have attained true peace of mind. Below is a short, and by no means complete, list of elements that are included when the American Dream is discussed:

Living the Dream
1. Go to a good school
2. Get a good job and work hard
3. Build a successful business
4. Own a home and enjoy it
5. Own a car and enjoy it
6. Have a family and enjoy time with them
7. Travel and leisure
8. Financial freedom
9. Comfortable Retirement

As you continue to grow and become more and more comfortable living in the United States, you will begin to see and experience so many other things that help you get closer and closer to the ultimate American Dream and the Pursuit of Happiness.

One thing that is critical is to remember the American Dream is a concept that needs nourishing. Stay humble and remember your basic understanding of common sense. As we say here in America, learn to walk before you run; that means to stay humble and learn every day to get better and better. There is always a risk of building the dream and seeing it go up in flames if you are not careful. Enjoy the life you have worked hard for, but save for the rainy days.

In Chapter 8, I will guide you, so you can continue to succeed by working hard and smart, gaining respect from your community, your friends, and relatives. In Chapter 9, I will show you step-by-step how to enjoy the fruit of your hard labor and sacrifice. You have made it—now is the time to live and thrive.

CHAPTER 8

Get to Work

In this chapter, I will offer you many tips on how to succeed once you are in the United States—and how hard and smart work make it possible for you to realize your American Dream. After these following chapters, you will be able to answer the question about the American Dream—namely, whether it is worth the price. Needless to say that just like the previous chapters, which focused on developing the right mindset, setting goals, learning the English language, keeping an open mind, and giving to the community and the country, this chapter is as critical to realizing your American Dream in the United States.

Hard Work

In the United States, there is a saying that goes like this: "To succeed in life, you have to work hard to get where you want to be."

Whether it is in school, at work, in running a business, or playing a sport, there is a lot to say about hard work and how it leads to success. In the United States, people value hard work and respect hard-working people. Hard work, the American

Dream, and the Pursuit of Happiness are closely related. One does not happen without the other. In addition to hard work, I strongly believe that smart work also can help in succeeding in many areas.

In school, it is imperative to put the requisite work in if you want to get good grades and graduate with a degree. Take it from me—I was in school for many years because I went on to get my Masters and Doctorate after I finished college. One has to study hard and put in the time and consistent efforts to do well and be rewarded with a degree. People with advanced degrees in many disciplines end up getting better jobs than those with no degrees. In addition to hard work, there are sacrifices made by serious students who spend hours studying and getting ready for tests and exams. Teachers and administrators in schools monitor students' work through the curricula and are responsible not only for grading students, but also for writing recommendations to advanced programs in good schools.

There are many examples I can share with you about friends from college who always studied the smart way—they attended the lectures regularly, prepared prior to the classes, asked the right questions, participated in the discussions, and got the teachers' attention.

But please remember, many folks argue that you don't have to have an advanced degree to succeed financially and realize your own American Dream.

At the workplace, the same is true about working hard and working smart. Coworkers and supervisors observe how you behave at work, and how hard and smart you do your work. In many jobs physical hard work may be required. In others, using your head and intellect may be more in demand to accomplish projects. How hard and how smart—and sometimes who you impress—make a difference in whether you get a salary increase, a promotion, both, or nothing at all.

Running a business is also a good example where both hard work and smart work lead to success. When you have your own business and your own employees and customers, you are in charge and responsible for how successful your company becomes. You monitor your employees and the work they do. You follow your customers and see how satisfied they are with your employees, your products, and services. Your employees also monitor how good of a boss you are.

At work and in business, many times you run into people who are workaholics, meaning that their work ALWAYS comes first. This can lead to success, but it also takes you away from family and friends. I recommend you balance your work life and your time with family and friends. There are many stories I can share with you about the sacrifices many Americans make—whether they spend many hours in their workplace or business or travel many days away from family.

In sports, we talk about the concept that "Practice makes perfect." This is a reference to how much time the best and most well-prepared athletes spend in practice, becoming exceptional at what they do. Players like Steph Curry in basketball, or Tiger Woods and many others in golf, are examples of how hard work and practice lead to success within one's sport. In sports, teammates, coaches, and team owners monitor your work and your attitude toward the sport and the fans. Fans closely monitor how you and your team perform, and that makes a profound difference on how many fans will follow you and how many tickets will be sold for your games at home and away.

Music and acting are also great examples of disciplines where practice makes perfect. Whether you are an actor, a pianist, a violinist, a guitar player, or a singer, the more time you spend rehearsing and practicing your trade, the better you become.

In all of those areas I have discussed, hard work and smart work will lead to success and rewards. Some of the most important elements to remember are:

1. Good Discipline - it means you show up on time to classes, to an appointment, to work, to practice, to a concert, to a game, or to any event where others are expecting you to be there. Vince Lombardi used to famously say that if you are on time, you are actually 15 minutes late. This ethos means show up 15 minutes early to any meeting, practice, or appointment.

2. Good Ethics - don't cheat yourself or others. Be fair and put in the work you are getting paid for, regardless of how small or large the work is.

3. Be the Best - strive for your top performance in anything you do. Give your best so that when your head hits the pillow at night, you know you have done well and have given it your best.

In the next few paragraphs, I will discuss the importance of being creative and working smart to be successful. Let's also take a look at how respecting and encouraging others while socializing can improve your chances of success and add to your hard and smart work.

Work Smart

There are many examples of immigrants who come to the United States, and whether because of education, wealth, or lack of both, end up either doing respectable white-collar jobs or hard blue-collar jobs. For example, millions of immigrants work in farming, landscaping, and construction. Some of the work is hard work, but the money is good in construction, for instance. Farming and landscape work is hard work, and the money is not always that good. It is all relative, of course.

There are also many great examples of successful immigrants who came to the United States and became well known for their genius, creativity, and skills. In the area of sports, (basketball, baseball, and soccer, to name a few) many have left their mark in their sports; some even went back to their native countries and built hospitals and schools, such as Mutombo, the basketball player. Others have become fashion gurus (Oscar de la Renta), body-building and movie celebrities (Arnold Schwarzenegger), and politicians (Madeleine Albright, the first woman Secretary of State).

When it comes to working smart, there are numerous examples of successful immigrants who parlayed their skills into becoming world-changing tech gurus. Look at the individuals who started Google, YouTube, eBay, and WhatsApp. All are great examples of immigrants who used their genius to create successful companies and went on to not just become wealthy, but to also generously donate great sums of money to help charities. They have helped many others become rich and created many jobs in the tech sector.

Despite all of these contributions to the country, the debate about immigration continues in the United States. This is the cause of dividing people in groups based on their ideology and political views. In many ways, this is nothing new in the American experience. My careful reading of American history has shown how anxieties over immigration have often boiled up, especially in times of economic anxiety in which citizens have looked for an easy scapegoat. Just look back at the history of "No Irish Need Apply" signs hung up in storefront windows.

There are those who are in favor of immigration and those who are against it. My recommendation is to ignore all of the noise. Stay focused on your goals and the ultimate success that is the American Dream. Taking sides on the immigration dilemma, especially if you are new in the country, may not benefit you and will not affect the outcome unless you can vote and participate in the process.

The best thing you can do to positively impact the immigrant debate is to personally strive to be the best citizen you can be. Some Americans may resent immigration in the abstract, until they forge close relationships with the immigrants in their communities and in their workplaces.

To improve your odds for success in the area of working smart, think about team work, whether it is in school, business, or sports. Learn to leverage the good skills from others around you. Many companies look for employees who are team players—the same with professional sport teams. If you are still in school, look for students who can help you study better and think better. Working in harmony with others can lead to great and beneficial discoveries for society in the area of technology, science, medicine, and many other disciplines.

You become an American not just by receiving benefits, but by contributing to your society and community. When you open up your perspective and look for solutions to problems, you contribute to making your world a better place for you, me and all others around—for our children and our grandchildren, and the many human generations to come.

Many well-known people became famous for their contribution to society. They used their intelligence, their creative thinking, and other skills to create many good technologies for the good of society. So, I encourage you to get involved and use your God-given talents and genius to do well and help realize your American Dream and the dreams of many others. I am proud of you already, and I know you will contribute anywhere you end up in the United States of America.

In the last part of this chapter, I will introduce you to some other areas that will help get you closer to your American Dream and the Pursuit of Happiness. By respecting others and helping them become successful, you will become successful and be rewarded immensely. Go for it and enjoy the ride.

Are you starting to feel the vibes and the breezes of the American Dream? It is approaching, and your time will come. Stay with me—you are almost there.

In Chapter 9, I will lay it all in front of you—your American Dream. You can tell me and the world whether the price is too high…or whether it is worth every penny, every tear, every sacrifice, and every minute away from your native land, family, and friends.

Respect and Rewards

You can work hard, you can work smart, and you can contribute to society. There will be difficult days and setbacks. But if you stay the course, you too can become successful—far more than you may have ever imagined...

But you still have to interact with people in your new community and your new country. To have successful interactions with others, you want to get their respect. If you want to be respected, you have to give respect. You must learn to encourage people and show appreciation for what they do. Do not judge, but listen and try to empathize, meaning you put yourself in their shoes. Armed with success and respect from others, you will be rewarded immensely, whether you are in school, at work, or just among others in the neighborhoods. Remember what we said about first impressions—people get their first impressions of you in the first ten seconds or less. So, remember to smile, take a deep breath, and enjoy the moment and the ride.

Respect Others

Here is a short list of ways to respect others and gain respect back

1. Show courtesy

2. Watch your language

3. Watch your manners

4. Watch how you approach men and women you don't know

5. Don't be rude

6. Don't interrupt
7. Listen
8. Give people space and time to respond
9. Be sensitive
10. Don't ask embarrassing questions
11. Learn to forget and forgive
12. Give others the benefit of the doubt
13. Don't be loud
14. Don't lie
15. Share your skills and your culture
16. Don't start fights
17. Don't engage in arguments whether you are right or wrong
18. Learn to say sorry and ask for forgiveness
19. Smile and say thank you

Encourage & Socialize

Just as you want to be encouraged by others and accepted in the community, others feel the same way, especially if they are new, like you, in the neighborhood. If you see someone trying hard at something, offer some encouraging words. If you see someone struggling, offer to help. Remember when we discussed times where you want to give before you receive? Treat people like you want to be treated.

Get involved in events in your community. Be the one to introduce yourself first. Here is a short list of events and places you can attend where you can meet others and socialize:

1. Neighborhood block parties
2. Home owner association meetings
3. Religious gatherings
4. Social outings
5. School activities
6. Company outings
7. Holiday parties
8. Beaches and parks
9. Restaurants
10. Grocery stores
11. Malls

Enjoy the Rewards

In the United States, people encourage each other. They cheer for each other, they applaud, and they make deafening noise at sporting events when there is a good play or a score. There are many awards given to winners in movies (think of the Oscars), theater, TV, and music. In schools, they recognize academic achievements and graduations. At work, people recognize promotions, inventions, and retirements. There are many occasions to celebrate, like birthdays, anniversaries, weddings, and more.

Learn to relax and go with the flow, as we say here. Enjoy the moment and the experience. Very soon, you will be awarded for being you and for being a winner. You will be recognized for your achievements and your hard work.

You came a long way, baby, and it is time for you to enjoy what you came here for—the American Dream and the Pursuit of Happiness.

By now, you have a good idea of what it feels like to be accepted and living with your new neighbors. In the final chapter, I will share with you what it feels like to live the American Dream and encourage you to continue to hope—to dream more and to enjoy. I will show how you can enjoy the fruit of your labor, hard work, and sacrifice. Then it will be time to decide your next move.

Is the American Dream alive and well? Is the price too high to pay? Would you stay and become a US citizen—or would you go back home and share the experience with others who may be dreaming of coming to the United States?

Get ready for the finale.

KEY CHAPTER 9

Time to Thrive

Are you ready for the Pursuit of Happiness and the American Dream? How do you feel now that you belong in this new society?

You came a long way. You sacrificed a lot. Now is the time to enjoy the fruit of your hard labor. You and your family will find happiness in your new home away from home. You are now living the American Dream.

Progress Report So Far

Let's see where you are now with school, if you came here to study; at work, if you are here to work and make a living.

Let's review how you are doing with communication in the community, and how you are coming along with your family and finances.

In this chapter, you will have the opportunity to learn how to evaluate progress and happiness for yourself and define what they mean to you. You will answer the ultimate question—whether the American Dream is for you.

Is it worth the sacrifice? Where do you go from here? Continue the journey and become more successful by staying here and starting a family? Go back home and share the experience with others who are dreaming about coming to the United States of America to visit, to study, to work, or to start a business? Is it your turn to write your story and share it with the world?

In my case, I came to study and go back home to practice medicine or teach at the university level. But after college and graduate school, I ultimately knew I wanted to stay here, find a job, and start a family. I have learned to adapt and live comfortably in the United States. I learned how to move around, communicate, and interact. I learned how it works to survive and thrive.

Even with advanced degrees from a reputable university like Fordham, it was not easy to find a job immediately. I was fortunate, however; I met a beautiful girl in New York, and we got married in 1983.

Connie was already living in California for about two years, working for IP—International Paper Co. I had already visited California and fallen in love with it. Let this serve as a reminder to enjoy your journey as it happens. Your journey will not unfold exactly how you have planned. Rather than obsess over every move you will make, take pleasure in the ride. Make every moment count. Make every moment a learning experience to further your progress. Enjoy and cherish every experience. Every learning experience will help you move forward, closer to your ultimate goal.

The American Dream: Are You Feeling It?

1. *Degree/Job*
2. *Home/Car/Bank Account*
3. *Family/Friends*/What's next?

It took me several months before I landed a real job with Cline Buckner in the spring of 1984.

I had been a broke student all my life; now a small company was offering me an annual salary of $33,000, a company car, and an expense budget. I felt rich beyond anything I could have ever imagined. I learned one thing about jobs—when you have no work experience, get what you can get and get good at it. When you get a chance to prove yourself, learn, do the best job you can do, and deliver. You will be noticed, and other companies will find you and offer you better jobs and salaries.

That is exactly what happened to me. I learned a lot from my first boss, the president of the company, my fellow employees, my customers, and our suppliers. I made friends and started to enjoy life with my wife.

At first, we lived in Connie's apartment in Irvine, CA. After a few months and some savings in our bank accounts, we bought a condo in Irvine as well. Connie was making good money, and my salary steadily bumped up. With the help of our savings, we bought our first house in Mission Viejo. That first house was a lovely model home located on Sierra Vista Street in Mission Viejo.

It was not long after that we purchased our first luxury car—a Mercedes Benz 300S in a smoked silver color, which Connie drove since I had a company car. We enjoyed living in Mission Viejo. Many relatives visited us often while we lived in California—Connie's late father, John Parrinello, my late mother, my sisters, and other relatives and friends from the East Coast and back home in Morocco.

In 1988, we were blessed with our first child. Ashley Nicole was born on August 11. Before that, we had Papillon, a Lhasa Apso, a beautiful dog.

I worked four years with Cline Buckner. In May of 1988, I was offered a job I could not refuse from Whitmire Research Labs, located in St Louis, Missouri. They were a competitor of Cline Buckner, and I had the right experience for the opportunity. At that time, it was one of the best family-owned companies to work for in the pest management business. After a few years with Whitmire, we moved to a larger home located on a 17-hole golf course in Dove Canyon Country Club. Talk about living the American Dream—both of us were working and making good money back then. We upgraded our personal car from a Mercedes Benz 300 to a beautiful white Mercedes Benz 400, then to a BMW. There was a Jeep Cherokee Laredo somewhere in there as well.

In 1992, we were blessed again with a second child—Jaclyn Michelle was born on July 25.

By this time, I was traveling quite a bit, and so was Connie for her work. Childcare was an ongoing challenge. Ashley and Jaclyn attended a Montessori School before moving to St. John's in Rancho Santa Margarita, where Dove Canyon was. I remember one time when both Connie and I had to be away for a week for company business. We could not find a babysitter for the week, so we flew to Brooklyn, where we left the girls with Connie's family, Grandpa John and Uncle Joe. Looking back at that period, it was a mixed feeling of happiness and a challenge to juggle work and family.

After years working for Whitmire, my old company, Waterbury Cos, who had acquired Cline Buckner, came calling and offered me a position as VP of Professional Products. It was a good base salary, and I would gain the opportunity to participate in the management stock option program. We had to relocate to Connecticut for that position. By that time, SC. Johnson had acquired Whitmire and merged it with Micro Gen; at this point, many employees, including myself, had cashed out our company shares.

The new management had a different philosophy of running the company compared to the way Blanton Whitmire used to run it. It was clearly time for me to move on. The opportunity to move to Connecticut was attractive, as we could be closer to family and relatives living in New York and New Jersey.

The idea of Connie staying home raising the girls was also another good reason to make the move, since my salary alone was going to be enough for us to live on.

After four years with Waterbury Cos, I left to start my own business. I had always wanted to start my own business. My goal was to do it when I turned 50—another story for another time. But so far, I have done well—and I am confident that you will do well too. Remember to enjoy the precious moments with your spouse and kids and friends as much as you can. Things change with time, and you may never experience the same moments again.

We had the best neighbors in Connecticut when we moved to our beautiful home on Copper Beach, Cheshire. We were one of the first families to build a home on that street, and we welcomed other families as they built their homes and moved to our street. We used to get together often with our neighbors, the Urbanos, the Mascas, and the Karluckis. The girls joined the

Cheshire Soccer Club and were enjoying the sport. I coached for several seasons, and Connie and I enjoyed being with the girls when they were playing at home or away. We had the best time with soccer in Cheshire. Great memories to cherish forever. Ashley eventually hurt her knee playing soccer and had to slow down and not play anymore. Jaclyn, who started playing while she was five, stayed with it and enjoyed playing in middle school and with the Cheshire soccer teams.

When we moved to GA, Jaclyn joined the Stars Soccer Club and played there for several years. She was also a member of the Milton Soccer Club and played several seasons. At Georgia University, she played intramural soccer and even coached at the soccer club in Athens, Georgia. She still enjoys playing whenever she can in California, where she works and lives.

To me, this is my American Dream. Next, I will ask you some questions regarding what's next for you.

Do you stay, or do you go back? Is the American Dream alive and well for you? Is the price too high to pay?

For me, the American Dream is alive and well. It is worth every penny and every tear. I would do it over again—and even better the second time around. I am a naturalized American citizen. I pay taxes and vote. My vote counts. I live in a democracy. Priceless.

Have You Found Happiness Yet? Freedom?

1. *Would you stay and live as a permanent resident?*
2. *When will it be time to go back home?*
3. *Not sure yet what to do?*

This is the moment of truth. You have come and conquered. You have learned so much from the previous chapters that you may consider yourself an expert. You may even be in a position to teach others how to succeed in America and realize their own American Dreams. You see, no matter the results, though we do consider them, the fun and the fulfillment are throughout the journey. As you learn, you find challenges and come up with solutions.

You fail, and you learn from your failures. To succeed in life is to find and create happiness in everything you do. When you reach your goal and realize your American Dream, you are content, you are satisfied, you are fulfilled, and then maybe you are compelled to want to do more, give more, and live better. You may decide to stay in the United States and become a great U.S. citizen. You may vote and help others live a better life and make this world a better place.

You may decide to go back home and be with your relatives and friends and take so many positive things with you and share them with others.

Maybe you are not sure what to do—and that is okay. Take your time and evaluate the pros and the cons. You are now armed with so many positive and constructive things you learned from this book. You are now fearless and can face this world and be a part of it. You are now knowledgeable and responsible for helping to make it a better world for you and for me—and for others around us, and for our children and their children, and the many generations to come. Keep this book and read it often. It will remind you of why you came here.

Share it with other immigrants and non-immigrants so they can all learn from it and benefit from it. Share this book with the world. It contains precious, practical guidance on how to succeed in the United States and how to chase your goals and reach the American Dream. You have learned about the American Dream, the Pursuit of Happiness, and what it takes to get there.

You have learned and mastered the art of developing the right mindset, writing down goals and plans. You have learned how critical learning the English language is for you to survive and thrive. You learned how important it is to keep an open mind and learn from others without judging them and their way of life.

You have learned how to assimilate and adapt quickly and smoothly in living in this new land. This book has offered you practical tips on many different topics, along with some common sense and a lot of wisdom. I have strived to offer you many positive aspects in how to stay excited, motivated, and enthusiastic—because it takes all of that to help you get to the American Dream.

I have enjoyed every minute guiding you and offering my best material and tools for you to succeed in the United States. Let me leave you with this last advice—after reading this book, you need to *act*, because Knowledge + Action = Success. Get up every morning and be fired up and ready to go.

You have been given the greatest opportunity to come to this beautiful country...do something great with it. Be happy and help many others be happy. Help them realize their dreams as I helped you realize yours. Help keep the American Dream alive and well.

Thank you for buying and reading and sharing this book with others. Thank you for the time you took to study the material in this book. I invite you to submit comments and thank you in advance for helping make this world a better place.

Keep hope alive. God bless you and God bless the United States of America—a land of Freedom, Justice, Democracy, and the land of Opportunity. Amen.

EPILOGUE

A Letter to a Friend

Hello friend,

I enjoyed every minute sharing my experience of 48 years living in the United States of America: as an immigrant, a student, a soccer player, a U.S. citizen, an employee, a business owner, a taxpayer, a home owner, a car owner, a husband, a father, and a neighbor.

I enjoyed showing the reader how to come to the United States from anywhere in the globe, regardless of background or the reason for making the journey. I also enjoyed showing the reader how to be prepared to succeed, survive, and thrive in the United States of America.

This is a land of opportunity, but also a complex country with many different ethnic groups, religious and political tendencies, and socioeconomic classes. I enjoyed offering you, step-by-step, the many ways and solutions that can be used and applied to reach your American Dream and the Pursuit of Happiness.

I wished I had such a guide back in 1970 when I was ready to travel to the United States to study. I wish I knew more about the country, the people, and the many ways offered in this book to do the right thing and fulfill the American Dream, successfully and safely. I am so happy to report that you are now well prepared and ready to make the journey to the United States of America. You are now armed with the best ideas and practical tips and solutions to use to reach your goals and live happily in the new land.

I selected some very important topics to cover here. The first two are all about developing the right mindset and setting written goals and plans. It is important that the immigrant has a clear picture of why he or she is going to the United States with precise written goals and plans to complete the mission of realizing the American Dream.

The next topic we covered had to do with learning the English language. People in The United States of America communicate with others using English everywhere, in every context—reading, writing, and speaking. If you are going to school, or plan on working for an American company or starting a business in the United States, English is critical for survival. We emphasize the importance of keeping an open mind and learning from anyone who will help you move your goals along.

In Chapters 7, 8, and 9, I offered a step-by-step approach on what to do and not to do on a daily basis. I put a lot of emphasis on hard work and smart work, because in the United States people love hard work and hard-working people. They will respect you and embrace you when you believe in hard work as they do. The levels of competition for jobs are so high that you have to prove yourself by working hard and smart to succeed. You must work hard, and you must play hard—this is an expression you hear from those who put in the work and also know how to enjoy the fruits of their labor.

I am so excited for you. You are ready to realize your American Dream. You can do it with all of the information and the knowledge from this book. All you have to do is act and follow the instructions, living every moment along the journey.

Citizenship and living here is such a privilege. You may decide to go back home after finishing school or after making enough money to take back home. If that is the case, you will carry with you all the memories of an unforgettable journey. It truly was a privilege for me to share my passion and my book with you.

Options for the Reader

As I mentioned earlier, you may decide to stay in the United States of America as a permanent resident. Further down the road, you may even qualify for U.S. citizenship. Or you may decide to go back home to start a business, work for the government, or work for a private company. Either way, you will be armed with some of the great tips and ideas shared in this book and prepared to do about anything you put your mind to. This book opens up so many doors and so many pathways and provides so many options for the reader.

Let's review some of the popular options available to the reader after finishing reading the book, depending on whether they decide to stay or go back home:

1. You are a student who decides to stay and apply for permanent residency
2. You are a student who decides to finish your studies and go back home to pursue a career

3. You are an employee who decides to stay as a permanent resident and later applies for U.S. residency

4. You are an employee who decides to go back home and pursue a career there

The same also applies if you have a friend or loved one who is seeking to come to the United States as well.

Whether as a student, an employee, or a business owner, if your friend stays permanently in the United States legally, and eventually applies for citizenship, he or she will be well prepared as a result of reading and following many of the recommendations laid in this book, to fulfill their ultimate goal of reaching and living the American Dream. In addition to obtaining a degree from a good school and getting a good job with a good company in the U.S. Also, when owning a business, a home, and a car, and making friends, your friend will be presented with one of the most rewarding experiences in life.

Your friend will belong. They will be accepted and live and thrive in a society where democracy, Freedom of Speech and religion, and justice for all are rights under the constitution of the United States of America. Your friend will experience the ultimate voting rights to bring about positive changes to the community, the country, and even the world. Your friend will have the best opportunity to start and raise a family.

By following the recommendations laid out in this book, your friend will be armed with the building blocks of a solid foundation for success. Whether it is learning the English language for better communication, developing the right mindset and setting goals, or learning to give back to the community and the country, these are all excellent strengths that employers are looking in hiring candidates.

These are all excellent strengths and qualities to use to inspire and mentor others. Learn how to be excited, motivated, enthusiastic, and positive. Learn to be organized and disciplined. These are all qualities that help when you are looking for a healthy relationship and when you are looking for a job. These qualities will help your friend stay focused on being disciplined with finances and other important living conditions so their credit rating is high, which allows for borrowing money to buy a home or a car.

If your friend decides to go back after graduating from a good, reputable school, or after working for an American company or running a business, they will be prepared to succeed at home too. They can share what they learned in the United States with others. They can also share their experiences living in this country, possibly even inspiring and helping others who dream to migrate to the USA.

Yes, what goes around comes around... you were given the opportunity to come to the United States and prosper. Now it is your turn to help others succeed and prosper. Just think of all the options available as a result of reading this book and following the recommendations discussed. Think of all the doors that are open to you and the many opportunities to explore and choose from.

I am fortunate and grateful that I can share this book and its contents with many other immigrants, so they can succeed in life and in business. Thank you for the opportunity. God bless you and God bless the United States of America.

The American Dream is alive and well. The price is not too

high to pay. It is worth every penny and every tear.

Friend, the time has come to say goodbye for now. We will meet again, I am sure. It has been a great honor and a wonderful experience to share the contents of this book with you. I have learned a ton, and I hope you have learned and received what I have promised to deliver.

I would like for you to do me one final favor—please take this book with you anywhere you go. Whenever you run into a challenge or a problem that seems to be unsolvable, read one of your favorite chapters and remember your own personal reasons for why you are here. Remember the pages where I stressed being creative and innovative to find solutions to problems. Remember to find others who have had similar problems and see how they solved them.

Yes, you can do what you set your mind to. Nothing is impossible.

As you embark on your American journey, I wish you a lot more than luck. I wish you faith, courage, and character.

When you are done reading this book, please read it again. Better yet, please read it in front of other immigrants who are dreaming of traveling to the United States of America—to visit, to study, to work, or to start a business.

You are the reason this book was written—so that good things are spread around. Please become a good ambassador and a good missionary; share this book and its contents with others so we all leave this world in a better place and in good hands. Follow the directions in this book and you will accomplish what you never thought could be accomplished. I have helped you develop the right mindset so that you are always excited, positive, and generous with your time and kindness.

I started this relationship with you and will always be by your side. I hope that you find your answers on your own—for it is in the journey that we discover the miracle and the mystery of life. I ask of you—no, I beg you—to keep an open mind and learn from others. Give of your time, wisdom, and skills so others can benefit and find peace and happiness.

This is a noble cause. I respect you and your dreams from the bottom of my heart. I want you to succeed. You have what you need in this book to help you transition from your home country to the new homeland quickly and smoothly. Go explore and discover and live. You are blessed with this wonderful opportunity.

I am blessed to share my mind, my heart, and my soul with you so you can succeed. Keep the hope alive.

Your friend,

Mohamed

Online Resources for Immigrant Entrepreneurs to the US

1. USCIS (United States Citizenship and Immigration Services)
   https://www.uscis.gov

2. Adopt an Immigrant Mindset to Advance Your Career
   https://hbr.org/2012/08/adopt-an-immigrant-mindset-to

3. Entrepreneurs Pathways (USCIS)
   https://www.uscis.gov/working-united-states/working-us

4. 5 Steps to Get the Right Mindset for Success
   https://www.inc.com/jessica-stillman/5-steps-to-get-the-right-mindset-for-success.html

5. A Guide to Goal Setting
   https://www.entrepreneur.com/article/188454

6. ESL/ELL Education: Interactive Websites for Learning
   https://researchguides.library.wisc.edu/c.php?g=177873&p=1169756

7. ESL: English as a Second Language (Free English Resources)
   https://www.rong-chang.com/

8. Study English Abroad For Free
   https://www.dreamstudiesabroad.com/articles/study-abroad-for-free

9. The Immigrant Learning Center
   http://www.ilctr.org/

10. New American Entrepreneurs: Resources for Immigrant Business Owners
    https://www.excelsiorgrowthfund.org/business_resources/New-American-Entrepreneurs-Resources-for-Immigrant-Business-Owners_193_resource.htm

11. Living the American Dream: From Immigrant to Entrepreneur
    https://www.huffingtonpost.com/julie-barnes/living-the-american-dream_b_9830370.html

12. A Guide For Future Immigrant Entrepreneurs
    https://www.forbes.com/sites/stuartanderson/2017/12/03/a-guide-for-future-immigrant-entrepreneurs/#50388cfc4f13

www.ingramcontent.com/pod-product-compliance
Lightning Source LLC
LaVergne TN
LVHW011724060526
838200LV00051B/3019